CW01034232

Dear reader,

Whether this is y
a while since yo.
Room, I would like to welcome you po...
a worldwide community of believers who engage in
daily prayer and devotional practice.

For over 80 years, our magazine has encouraged
people everywhere to share their stories of faith.
Today it is published in more than 30 languages and is
found in over 100 countries. *The Upper Room* is used
by individuals, churches, small groups, chaplains and
community centres around the globe.

This special edition is designed to give you a sense
of how *The Upper Room* can contribute to your life
and to your community. It contains 31 meditations
written by ordinary people who have encountered
God in daily situations. It also includes small-group
discussion questions, tips for submitting your writing
to *The Upper Room*, and information about ordering
copies for yourself and others. Whether you choose
to use this for your ministry or for individual practice,
we hope you will find inspiration and resources for
growing closer to God.

Lindsay L. Gray

Editorial director
The Upper Room
Nashville, Tennessee

What readers say

'I very much appreciate reading the contributions from so many different places, and indeed so many different cultures.'

'I love the varied stories and choice of Bible passages. I look forward to my quiet time with God each day, using these notes. They also guide and widen my prayer horizon. Thank you.'

'I feel so enriched… reading people's personal experiences born from lives of faith, not simply doctrine or cold dogma.'

'I start every day with *The Upper Room*, my Bible, and my prayer list. Just like my father did.'

'Like is an understatement – I am in love with *The Upper Room* daily devotional!'

 Ministries

15 The Chambers, Vineyard
Abingdon OX14 3FE
brf.org.uk

Bible Reading Fellowship is a charity (233280)
and company limited by guarantee (301324),
registered in England and Wales

ISBN 978 1 80039 233 5

Originally published in the USA by The Upper Room® upperroom.org

The contents of this publication were first published in *The Upper Room* between 2014 and 2022.

A catalogue record for this book is available from the British Library

Printed by Zenith Media

Good connections

Read Galatians 3:24–29

'My prayer is not for them alone. I pray also for those who will believe in me through their message, that all of them may be one.'
John 17:20–21 (NIV)

Reading an *Upper Room* devotional written by a woman from Russia helped me think about the greatness and goodness of God. I wondered, *What family does she have? Does she work outside the home? What is her daily life like?* I prayed for her and marvelled at the connection we have through our faith in the Lord, even though we live thousands of miles apart.

This bond of faith happens each day in my devotional time as I read *The Upper Room*. The writer for the day may be from England or Ethiopia, from Australia or the United States, or from anywhere else in the world. The experiences and insights they write about always help me in some way and strengthen my faith. I pray for those who share their faith in writing and also for those who work to bring this magazine into publication.

We can also feel a strong bond with those closest to us — those in our neighbourhood, our church, our families and at work. The apostle Paul wrote, 'Clothe yourselves with love, which binds everything together in perfect harmony' (Colossians 3:14, NRSV). No matter where we live, God's love urges us to love one another and gives us the enduring joy of knowing that we are connected to God and to others by love and faith.

Prayer: *Thank you, God, for your gracious love for us that enables us to connect with one another. Amen.*

Thought for the day: We are connected to one another through God's love.

Joan S. Hutcheson (Georgia, USA)

PRAYER FOCUS: THE STAFF AND WRITERS OF *THE UPPER ROOM*

The old watch

Read Joshua 24:14–17

Cast all your anxiety on him, because he cares for you.
1 Peter 5:7 (NRSV)

As a minister, I recently received an appointment to a new congregation. I was packing and waiting for the big change in my life when I saw my grandmother's old watch, which she had received from her father. It was more than 60 years old and still working.

The evening before leaving my home for the last time, I thought about my life and recalled the life of my grandmother. The old watch had counted out her hours in this world and the hours of her father's life, and I know it was counting out the hours of my life as well, a life I enjoy as a gift from God. And I thought, *What will my service be like? What example will I leave behind?* I remembered the words of Psalm 90:12: 'So teach us to count our days that we may gain a wise heart.'

We do not have much time in this world; we do not know when the hands of our life's watch will stop. But what we do know is that our loving God has given us life and the ability to choose how we will live it. May our lives be full of faith, hope and love for all that God has created!

Prayer: *Dear God, lead us on your way and give us wise hearts so we can remain faithful to you, our loving creator. Amen.*

Thought for the day: How am I showing gratitude for the life God has given me?

Vladimir Angelov (Ruse, Bulgaria)

Word of life

Read Romans 8:1–4

'If you love me, you will keep my commandments.'
John 14:15 (NRSV)

I was not excited to hear that the Ten Commandments were to be our topic of study for the next few weeks. I thought, 'Surely, as we are now in the New Testament era, all these laws are behind us?'

Then I recalled reading about a man who became a Christian while in prison. When he was released, he went into a church for the first time in his life. On the wall, in large letters, were listed the Ten Commandments. His heart sank. He had thought he had been set free, but now, how could he keep all those 'Thou shalt nots'? He brought his despair in prayer to Jesus, and when he looked again, they seemed to read differently. Instead of 'Thou shalt not...', he read them as 'You won't...'

If we come to Jesus as Lord and Saviour, we too will find that not only are our sins forgiven, but also we are given new life in Christ; not only are we are released from condemnation, but also we are empowered by the Holy Spirit to live a life of love that is the fulfilment of the law (see Romans 13:10).

As week by week we have been studying these ten wonderful commands, we have been seeing them now, in the light of Jesus' salvation, not as a means by which God condemns us, but a pattern of the life God enables us to live. How wonderful is God's love for us!

Prayer: *Lord, please help us to love you with all our hearts and to allow you to love our neighbours through us.*

Thought for the day: Through the Spirit, I have God's laws written on my heart.

Pauline Lewis (Wales, United Kingdom)

Loving our neighbours

Read Matthew 2:7–12

'No one has greater love than this, to lay down one's life for one's friends.'
John 15:13 (NRSV)

While serving in Iraq in 2007, I awoke early one morning with an overwhelming feeling of dread. I prayed desperately that God would protect me and shield my family from the pain they would experience if I didn't return home. I wrote a letter to my wife and children and asked my operations officer to ensure my family received it if something happened to me.

Despite fear that made me sick to my stomach, we set out on our mission. On the outskirts of Baghdad, we were halted by the frantic Muslim chief of police with whom I had been working for over a year. He insisted we go no further because the road ahead was arrayed with roadside bombs. After further investigation we found that we had been set up for an attack, and our deaths had been averted by this unexpected messenger.

I still struggle with thoughts of that day, but I take comfort in the friendship that God placed in my path through that devoted and honest man. It would have been easy for him to let us drive past or for me to ignore his warning. My unlikely friend taught me a lesson about love and kindness that day. Our neighbours are often very different from us. God calls us to seek friendship, kindness and understanding even from those who appear different. Loving all our neighbours opens us up to great blessings.

Prayer: *Heavenly Father, teach us to show kindness to strangers. Help us to treat others the way we want to be treated and to embrace all people as your children. Amen.*

Thought for the day: God calls me to show kindness to everyone I meet.

Chad B. McRee (Texas, USA)

A way out

Read 1 Corinthians 10:8–13

God is faithful; he will not let you be tempted beyond what you can bear. But when you are tempted, he will also provide a way out so that you can endure it.
1 Corinthians 10:13 (NIV)

Anxious to get home after a long day at work, I rushed through the grocery store and did not notice that the cashier had accidentally given me extra change. As I neared the exit, I caught the mistake, and thoughts started streaming in my mind: *Walk faster. No one will know.* Then another thought followed: *This must be a test.*

This last thought began to consume me because this had been the second such experience I'd had that day. Earlier, I had almost left a public bus without paying for the fare; but then I felt that God was telling me that if I went on and didn't pay, I would be sinning. If instead I went back to pay, I would be growing and maturing for the glory of God. I paid my bus fare and ultimately gave back the extra change to the cashier as well.

Being short on money and yet having two challenges involving money in one day reminded me of the way temptations sometimes storm our lives and cloud our judgement to the extent that we start viewing things that are wrong as right. But God is faithful and knows us and never stops giving us instruction and reproof to help us endure temptation.

Prayer: *Mighty God, thank you for delivering us from temptations today. In Jesus' name. Amen.*

Thought for the day: Today, with every temptation, I will look to God for the way out.

Vimbai Chizarura (Mashonaland East, Zimbabwe)

Thinking ahead

Read 2 Peter 1:3–9

*Forgetting what is behind and straining towards what is ahead,
I press on towards the goal to win the prize for which God has called
me heavenwards in Christ Jesus.*
Philippians 3:13–14 (NIV)

A little girl had just returned home after visiting an elderly lady with her mother. 'Mummy,' she said, 'when I am an old lady I want to be like that lovely lady.' 'In that case,' replied her mother, 'you'd better start practising now, because it takes a very long time.'

What are we aiming for in life? What kind of people do we hope to become? Our answer to those questions affects our thinking, our attitude, our speech and our actions, and determines the way we develop as Christians.

When we read 2 Peter 1:3–9, we find that the way to develop Christian character is a step-by-step process, starting from the time we come to Christ right through to the end of our life. As we learn of Jesus in God's word, listen to him as we pray and obey him, he continues to gradually change us. It doesn't happen automatically; it needs serious commitment from us and we shouldn't expect it to be easy.

Do we want to be like Jesus? Then we must start practising now, because it is a lifetime's work. Young or old, new believer or long-time Christian, let us, as the apostle Paul wrote, press on right to the end of our life's journey towards that goal.

Prayer: *Help us, Lord, today and every day, to keep our aim before us, so that we may keep growing to be more like Jesus. Amen.*

Thought for the day: I will give my utmost for his highest.

Hazel V. Thompson (England, United Kingdom)

Visiting Will

Read John 6:43–48

*'I have placed before you an open door that no one can shut. I know
that you have little strength, yet you have kept my word and have not
denied my name.'*
Revelation 3:8 (NIV)

I remember the sound of the gravel under my tyres as I drove up the
lane to visit my friend Will. I can still see him waving from his porch –
one arm extended and the other leaning on his cane. 'What took you so
long?' he'd ask.

'I stopped to ask a deer for directions.' This joke always made him
laugh. We'd sit and talk about nature, his kids and how the stroke had
made him angry and less motivated. I mostly listened. He just needed to
be heard. Will had a long history of drug abuse, alcoholism, wrong turns
and pain that he carried deep inside.

I visited Will for about a year and watched him grow weaker over time.
He wouldn't talk about God. 'That isn't for me. I am good where I'm at,'
he'd say. One rainy afternoon, as I pulled into Will's drive, he walked
unsteadily towards me through the tall grass to welcome me. 'I did it!'
he exclaimed.

'Did what?' I asked.

'You know — went down to the ol' church and got right.' I smiled and
shook my head with an awesome feeling of fulfilment. We chuckled and
walked back to his porch. In the last months of Will's life, the Holy Spirit
had called him to walk through the church doors and forever be with God.

Prayer: *Heavenly Father, thank you for opportunities to share your
love and grace with others. Amen.*

Thought for the day: My small actions can make a huge difference in
someone's life of faith.

Matt Simmons (Kentucky, USA)

An easy plan to use *The Upper Room* in small groups

Christ said that where two or three gather in his name, he is present (see Matthew 18:20). In each issue of *The Upper Room*, questions are included for small groups to gather and discuss the Wednesday readings. This offers believers an easy way to share a longer devotional time together on a regular basis. It is recommended that groups:

- Begin by reading the Bible passage on the Read line and the day's meditation, allowing silence for at least a minute afterward. Then ask members to turn to the questions for that date listed below or on one of the following pages.

- Ask someone to read aloud the questions one by one, giving each member the opportunity to answer after each question. If anyone prefers not to answer a question, move on to the next person.

- Discuss how everyone thinks differently, and try to hear what the Holy Spirit may be saying to you in all this.

- Decide what you will do with God during the week.

- Be quiet and pray together.

For a more detailed meeting guide, see **upperroom.org/resources/a-guide-for-small-groups**. The following are study questions to accompany a few of this issue's readings.

Day 7   Visiting Will

1   Describe a time when your small actions made a big difference for someone. How did this experience encourage you?

2   Who in your life, like Will, simply needs to be heard? How will you make sure this person knows that you hear and love them?

3   Today's writer witnesses through his actions, rather than always talking about God. Is it always beneficial to witness primarily through actions or does it depend on the situation?

4   Will said, 'That isn't for me. I am good where I'm at.' Have there been times in your life when you've felt a similar way about God? What caused you to feel this way, and what brought you back to God?

Day 20   Taking a risk

1   When have you decided to take a risk that others did not understand or tried to discourage you from taking? Did their concerns make you think differently about your decision? Did you take the risk after all?

2   Can you relate to the writer's experience of feeling called by God to a particular place or kind of work? How do you listen for God's guidance? What practices help you to determine God's will for your life?

3   Do you think others can see your faith in your actions and decisions you make? If so, how? If not, how can you help others see that your faith informs your daily decisions?

4   Today's writer says that we sometimes need to take risks to make ourselves available to God. When has this been true in your experience?

Day 27   Ebenezer

1   If you were to make a list of ten things that you are thankful for today, what would your list include?

2   Have you ever been in a situation where it was hard to sense God's faithfulness? How would you encourage someone going through a similar experience? What would you do differently were you to be in a situation like that again?

3   Name some passages of scripture that illustrate God's faithfulness to us. Which of these is your favourite? What parallels do you see between the ways God helped the people in scripture and the ways God helps you in your life today?

4   When on your walk of faith have you struggled with doubt? What helped you overcome your doubt? Is it okay to have times in our lives when we doubt God's faithfulness?

Being accountable

Hebrews 10:23–25

We urge you, brothers and sisters, to admonish the idlers, encourage the fainthearted, help the weak, be patient with all of them.
1 Thessalonians 5:14 (NRSV)

I went mountain climbing the other day and met up with some energetic students. When I thought I could not possibly go on, they shouted words of encouragement: 'You can do it!' 'You are one strong lady!' 'This is nothing. You've made it this far; the worst is over.' At times, they burst into song to boost morale. Together, we made it all the way.

This experience reminds me of our Christian walk. Sometimes the battle is too fierce, and we feel we can't go on. We don't have the strength even to pray. In such times, we need other people to support, encourage and admonish us in love. Through Christian fellowship, we have the strength to hold on to God's sure promises and to continue. Being accountable to one another keeps us on track.

Some people say they need not go to church anymore because they listen to sermons on TV or on the Internet. This practice is no substitute for Christian fellowship. The TV won't comfort us through hard times, rejoice in our blessings or keep us accountable. Our brothers and sisters in Christ will.

Prayer: *Thank you, dear God, for the fellowship of believers. Teach us to cherish it and to play our roles in the community of faith. Amen.*

Thought for the day: We are members of the body of Christ and accountable to one another.

Veronica Kamidi (Nairobi, Kenya)

Special gifts

Read 1 Peter 4:8–11

Each of you should use whatever gift you have received to serve others, as faithful stewards of God's grace in its various forms.
1 Peter 4:10 (NIV)

My mother had the gift of hospitality. Even when we had very little money, she would whip up a spaghetti dinner with lots of steaming pasta and flavourful sauce and just enough juicy meat to add flavour. Then she would make a big green salad and a lovely cake. At times we would have as many as 15 people squeezed into our tiny home for a meal. I've tried to imitate her way of hosting people, but I feel inadequate. I admire my mother's way of showing hospitality; it's just not my gift.

However, I have taught English to a classroom of 30 adults from other countries, including some that did not speak any language that I know. I have taught Spanish, American Sign Language and Bible classes as well. Teaching is my gift. As long as I can feed people information instead of food, I do well. Once I quit trying to imitate my mother and started using the gifts God gave me, I relaxed and became more confident. Over time I have realised that we each have unique abilities that we can use to serve God and others.

Prayer: *Dear Lord, help us to recognise the special abilities that you have instilled in us and to use them in service to you. Amen.*

Thought for the day: I am unique with special gifts from God.

Mary Hunt Webb (New Mexico, USA)

The hope of refuge

Read Matthew 2:13–15

'I was hungry and you gave me food to eat. I was thirsty and you gave me a drink. I was a stranger and you welcomed me.'
Matthew 25:35 (CEB)

We have many refugees in our world today. Some flee civil war or violence. Others have seen their homes destroyed by natural disaster or have experienced the devastation of the infrastructure and industry of their community. The number of refugees saddens many of us, especially because refugees are not always welcomed with open arms.

In the Bible we read about one refugee family in particular – Mary, Joseph and the baby Jesus. If they had not fled their country seeking refuge, the baby would have been killed by King Herod's order. Many present-day refugees also face certain death if they remain in their own country. Even when they leave, the danger is not over. They face a perilous journey to other lands.

Mary and Joseph were able to return to their homeland after Herod died and the danger had passed. Many of today's refugees hope for the same result: they dream of when they might return home.

Those of us who have not been displaced can hope and pray for peace that will allow all refugees to return to their homelands. While we pray, we can also heed Christ's call to welcome the stranger. As Christians, we are called to do all we can for the refugees on our doorstep.

Prayer: *God of peace, keep us ever mindful of Jesus' teachings and that when we care for others, we honour him. Amen.*

Thought for the day: How open are my arms to God's people seeking refuge?

Bill Findlay (Scotland, United Kingdom)

A snake, a Bible and me

Read Lamentations 3:22–26
Your word is a lamp for my feet, a light on my path.
Psalm 119:105 (NIV)

Every morning that summer it was just me, my Bible and a snake. I had flown 750 miles across the country to work at a summer camp. While it was a remarkable place, I couldn't shake the feeling of loneliness. On the outside, I was the typical camp counsellor – hair smelling of chlorine, legs glistening in the 40-degree heat, wearing a smile from sunup to sundown. But the truth was, I had never wanted so badly to go home.

And yet, when I felt emptiest, God blessed me through a piece of paper someone gave me shortly before I arrived: a list of 100 verses of scripture to memorise.

Every dawn I would wake up before the campers, carefully avoid the armadillo as I hopped off the porch and find the same spot at the edge of the lake. I would unfold the list, welcome the snake who had moseyed to the rock opposite me and open my Bible. Never have I had a more peaceful, life-lifting time with God.

Often since then, those verses have popped into my mind – relieving me from anxiety, holding me back from temptation, guiding me towards a solution, reminding me to pray. Recalling those hours with God has been a constant reminder of the peace only God can provide.

Prayer: *Dear God, thank you for meeting us today and every day. We need you more than the bread we eat and the air we breathe. Amen.*

Thought for the day: God is good to me – all the time.

Melissa Ferguson (Tennessee, USA)

Restore with love

Read Colossians 3:12–14

Be completely humble and gentle; be patient, bearing with one another in love.
Ephesians 4:2 (NIV)

I recently read an article about a tribe in northern Natal in South Africa. According to tribal custom, when someone does something wrong or detrimental to others, the members of the tribe take the offender to the centre of the village and surround him or her. During two days, the tribe members tell the offender the good things he or she has accomplished. The purpose of the ritual is to restore the person and to affirm that he or she is essentially a good person.

I think that too often our tendency is to treat others unkindly, especially when they have made a mistake. We make sure to remind them continuously of their errors. Even in raising our children, we tend to emphasise the negative rather than the positive.

However, the Bible teaches love. In Matthew 22:39, Jesus says, 'Love your neighbour as yourself.' Galatians 6:1 reminds us, 'If someone is caught in a sin, you who live by the Spirit should restore that person gently.' Let us treat others the way we want to be treated. In doing so, we'll follow the example of Jesus, who loves us, even though we do not merit it.

Prayer: *Loving God, we confess that we are not perfect. Forgive us and teach us to follow your example of mercy. Amen.*

Thought for the day: Surrounding people with love can bring healing and restore community.

Narda Vargas (Dominican Republic)

The Livermore light bulb

Read Matthew 5:14–16

God, who said, 'Let light shine out of darkness,' made his light shine in our hearts.
2 Corinthians 4:6 (NIV)

Fire station #6 in Livermore, California, draws visitors from all over the globe. They come to see the world's most famous light bulb, a 60-watt bulb installed in 1901 which has been shining for over 115 years. That light bulb continues to baffle scientists, who can't explain how it has managed to glow for so long. Physicists discovered that the bulb's filament, the heart of the bulb, is about eight times thicker than that of an ordinary bulb, giving it extraordinary durability. Also, since a bulb which is turned on and off will typically have a much shorter lifespan, the fact that this bulb shines 24 hours a day is part of the secret.

That light bulb in Livermore is a tangible reminder for me that if we consider the words of Jesus, we'll want to let others see the loving light of God constantly shining through us.

Like the filament in that bulb, God calls us to radiate light continuously, year after year. Jesus said, 'You are the light of the world,' and 'Let your light shine before others, that they may see your good deeds and glorify your Father in heaven' (Matthew 5:14, 16). It is our privilege to glorify God and to share God's light with others so they may glorify God as well.

Prayer: *Jesus, light of the world, help us to share your light of love with those who pass through our lives. Amen.*

Thought for the day: How will I glorify God today?

Steven Cohen (California, USA)

The gift of emotions

Read Luke 19:41–46

As he approached Jerusalem and saw the city, he wept over it.
Luke 19:41 (NIV)

Growing up, I often experienced negative consequences when I expressed my feelings. So I dampened my exuberance and stifled my anger and sadness, hoping to make life easier. Unfortunately, numbing my emotions through overeating eventually led to obesity and the host of social and health challenges that accompany that condition.

Then I began to notice how Jesus displayed his feelings in scripture. He experienced the full range of human emotion: anger with the money-changers in the temple (John 2:15), grief over the death of his friend Lazarus (John 11:35) and joy in teaching his disciples (John 15:11).

Jesus allowed himself to be fully, deeply human whether in joy or suffering. This observation gave me the courage to begin to 'feel my feelings' while in the safety of Jesus' presence in prayer. Gradually, I was able to experience my feelings as they occurred and to understand them as good gifts from God.

Expressing our emotions is part of the abundant life to which Jesus invites us. When we express ourselves authentically, it is a gift to God, to ourselves and to the world.

Prayer: *Dear God, help us to continue to learn and grow so that we may be more effective in our ministries. Amen.*

Thought for the day: What emotional risk can God empower me to take today?

Margaret Gillikin (Colorado, USA)

A good foundation

Read 1 Corinthians 3:5–11

No one can lay any foundation other than the one that has been laid; that foundation is Jesus Christ.

1 Corinthians 3:11 (NRSV)

I grew up in a small rural village in Gujarat, India. For primary school, my parents sent me to a Christian boarding school. Though I received a good education, the school was not funded properly, and we never had enough to eat. I cannot think of a day during my four years at the school when I did not go to bed hungry. But when I look back, I have very fond memories of the school. During my years at the school, I came to know the Lord; and my education built a good foundation for the rest of my life.

Because I am so grateful for the seeds of faith that the school gave me, I have made a commitment to visit the school every year to help the children meet some of their needs. I provide a good meal and a small, practical gift for each child. After the meal, the children greet me and receive their gifts.

Each child hugs me and says, 'Thank you, Uncle. God bless you.' Being able to help the children of the school where the seeds of faith were first planted in me is one of the greatest joys and blessings of my life.

In today's reading, Paul reminded the Corinthian church that seeds of faith can be planted in many ways, but it is God who 'gave the growth' (v. 6). When we show compassion and nurture the faith of others, we help to lay the foundation of Christ for future generations.

Prayer: *God, our Father, be gracious to us and give us generous hearts that we may share with those in need. Amen.*

Thought for the day: How can I share my blessings with someone who needs them today?

Ishwarbhai Hirabhai Dabhi (Gujarat, India)

How can your ministry use *The Upper Room*?

- **Spiritual formation:** *The Upper Room* is an affordable, approachable resource for daily spiritual practice.

- **Small groups:** Each week, thoughtful discussion questions provide easy, self-guided content for participants to engage, reflect and grow.

- **Outreach:** Ministries around the world have provided *The Upper Room* to local hospitals, libraries, coffee shops, areas of refuge and prisons with information about their own ministry. These copies have sparked important conversations centered on Christ.

- **Diversity and inclusion:** *The Upper Room* intentionally includes writings from readers who represent all ages, genders and ethnic identities from around the world, allowing insight and connection among believers from all walks of life.

- **Leadership development:** *The Upper Room* supports the spiritual growth of leaders by giving them an easy way to connect with God through scripture and community.

Helping to pay it forward

As part of our Living Faith ministry, we're raising funds to give away copies of Bible reading notes and other resources to those who aren't able to access them any other way, working with food banks and chaplaincy services, in prisons, hospitals and care homes.

If you've enjoyed and benefited from our resources, would you consider paying it forward to enable others to do so too?

Make a gift at **brf.org.uk/donate**

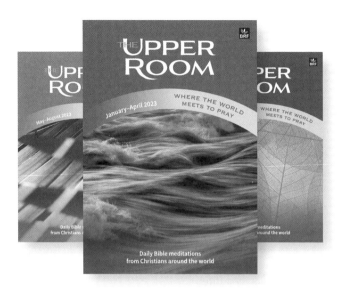

How to order *The Upper Room*

The Upper Room has a worldwide readership of some three million and is unique in that all the meditations are written by readers of *The Upper Room*, who seek to share the insights of their faith with others, thus providing a personal take on each passage and a different style each day.

Each daily meditation includes a recommended Bible reading and key verse (you will need a Bible), a reflection and a prayer. Questions for small group study are also included for each week.

The Upper Room is published three times a year, in January, May and September, and can be purchased as an annual subscription or single issue. To order your subscription, please use the order form on page 40, go to **brfonline.org.uk** or telephone the BRF office on +44 (0)1865 319700 (Monday to Friday, 9.30 am to 5.00 pm).

Like a forest

Read Romans 15:1–7

Accept one another… just as Christ accepted you, in order to bring praise to God.
Romans 15:7 (NIV)

As my husband and I drove through the forest to our campsite, I studied the trees along the road. One had some dead branches, another a broken top; still others had bent limbs or odd shapes. In fact every tree seemed to have some imperfection – yet together they formed a vibrant, green forest full of life. They provided shade for ferns and orchids and homes for any number of animals – from tiger swallowtail butterflies to white-tailed deer. And they gave us a peaceful place to camp and enjoy nature. Even the dead trees had a specific purpose; they were rotting into compost to nourish younger plants.

That forest reminded me of the people who make up God's church. We all have scars and imperfections. We make mistakes. Yet together we can form something beautiful.

We can bring forgiveness to the broken, strengthen the tempted and pick up the fallen so that they – in turn – can do the same for us. Instead of condemning those who make mistakes, we can offer a listening ear and a helping hand.

Together we can become a community that serves God and helps those in need while strengthening one another.

Prayer: *Dear God, help us to accept others and love them as you do, despite their imperfections – and despite our own. Amen.*

Thought for the day: Though we are scarred and imperfect, God builds the church with us.

Susan Thogerson Maas (Oregon, USA)

In God's hands

Read Psalm 31:9–16

My times are in your hands.
Psalm 31:15 (NIV)

I used to feel pressured by time constraints and would drive hurriedly, trying to beat traffic lights or pass other drivers. One day when things weren't going my way and everything seemed to frustrate my attempts to save time, a thought came to me: *Your time is in God's hands.* I relaxed and drove more slowly and considerately. Surprisingly, I arrived on time.

I have seen proof of my time being in God's hands in other ways as well. When I give my time to God in the morning by worshipping, through devotions like *The Upper Room*, I find that God seems to stretch my time, and I get things done more easily and with less effort than on the days when I don't worship this way.

Our time is truly in God's hands.

Prayer: *God of all times and places, receive our praise and gratitude as we see your work in our lives. We pray as Jesus taught us, saying, 'Our Father which art in heaven, Hallowed be thy name. Thy kingdom come, Thy will be done in earth, as it is in heaven. Give us this day our daily bread. And forgive us our debts, as we forgive our debtors. And lead us not into temptation, but deliver us from evil: For thine is the kingdom, and the power, and the glory, forever. Amen' (Matthew 6:9–13, KJV).*

Thought for the day: Today I will trust God with my time.

Carol S. Marti (Galicia, Spain)

Called by name

Read Isaiah 43:1–3

Do not fear, for I have redeemed you; I have called you by name;
you are mine.
Isaiah 43:1 (NRSV)

Some years ago, I accompanied a group of school students on a trip to the World War I battlefields in Belgium. We walked through trenches, imagining what it was like to be knee-deep in mud. We looked across a sea of white headstones in a beautifully kept British cemetery. We heard the last post and kept two minutes silence at the Menin Gate in Ypres. I remembered my great-uncle who had died at the Battle of the Somme in 1916. The students shared their family stories.

Now we were at Langemark, a German cemetery where over 44,000 young men were buried; 25,000 of these were in a mass grave about the size of a tennis court. There were no headstones; just grave markers laid flat on the cold earth. Most of the soldiers had no name to mark their last resting place. It was a bleak autumn day with oak leaves thick upon the ground.

I knelt beside the communal grave and brushed the leaves from the inscription: *Ich habe dich bei deine Name gerufen. Du bist mein.* ('I have called you by your name. You are mine.')

I no longer thought of an anonymous enemy but only of young men, little older than those in our group, known by name and loved by God.

Prayer: *Lord of all, may we love our enemies and pray for those who persecute us, for Jesus' sake. Amen.*

Thought for the day: God's love extends beyond human boundaries.

Andrew Dutton (England, United Kingdom)

Peace sign

Read Philippians 4:1–9

Bring up all of your requests to God in your prayers and petitions, along with giving thanks. Then the peace of God that exceeds all understanding will keep your hearts and minds safe in Christ Jesus.
Philippians 4:6–7 (CEB)

I started running for exercise at the age of 55. Since I live on a farm, I do most of my running on farm lanes or rural roads. I rarely see a car; but when I do, I always wave. My favourite vacation spot is Chincoteague, Virginia, where I must run in town amid tourist traffic. I still wave, even though a few of the drivers make little or no effort to slow down or move over, which would provide me a safe route to run.

This quickly started affecting me. I found myself getting agitated and angry, not just with a particular driver but with all drivers. Then I hit upon an idea. Instead of waving to drivers, I give the peace sign to wish them the peace of God. I pray for each driver and passenger that I encounter, especially the ones who don't slow down or move over.

I may not be able to make someone drive more safely, but when I pray for them the peace of God comes to me as well. Whenever we are tempted to lash out in anger, we can remember that in Christ we have found peace – a peace that we can share with everyone we encounter.

Prayer: *Dear God of peace, we thank you for creating a beautiful world for us to enjoy. Help us to appreciate the people of this world and to do our part to bring them your peace. In Christ's name we pray. Amen.*

Thought for the day: Instead of dwelling on my anger, I will pray.

Lynwood Broaddus (Virginia, USA)

PRAYER FOCUS: SOMEONE WHO HAS MADE ME ANGRY

Taking a risk

Read Matthew 5:11–16

Let your light so shine before men, that they may see your good works, and glorify your Father which is in heaven.
Matthew 5:16 (KJV)

At the age of 19 I felt God gently nudging me to join a mission organisation where I would attend a full-time discipleship training school. I was at a point of desperation to truly discover the God I had said I knew for the previous ten years, and this seemed just the ticket. I was ready to give up everything for this opportunity, but no one else in my life agreed with me. They said, 'How do you know it is God nudging you?' and 'You have a great job!' and 'What will you do after that?' Everyone had questions that seemed to imply they thought I had lost my mind.

But I had a peace in my heart about this idea, and I knew it had come from God. That was all I needed to hold on to when nothing else seemed to make sense. Following God's guidance leaves me happier and more fulfilled. When I'm at peace with my choices and I'm following God's will, my light shines. Other people see it and ask what I'm doing right.

Sometimes to make ourselves available to God, we have to take risks. Sometimes those risks take us out of our comfort zone. But it's in the dimness of the uncomfortable unknown that our lights shine best!

Prayer: *Dear God, help us to be ready to go where you call us and to trust your guidance so that our lights will shine before others. Amen.*

Thought for the day: Even if others question me, I will be ready to answer God's call.

Amorelle Reneisha Browne (Grenada)

Ordinary heroes

Read 1 Corinthians 1:26–31

God chose what the world considers low-class and low-life – what is considered to be nothing – to reduce what is considered to be something to nothing.
1 Corinthians 1:28 (CEB)

In popular literature, plays and poetry, the common people often have unimportant roles, while the exalted parts go to kings, princes and princesses. But the New Testament flips that perception. In God's story, the common people take centre stage. It is not a king's eloquent decree that makes Jesus stop, but rather a blind beggar who desperately calls out his name. As others rushed by this man, Jesus saw his value. The widow who donated only two copper coins is a heroine (see Mark 12:41–44). Jesus did not ignore the common people or portray them as buffoons.

In the gospels, we read about the nameless in 'the prodigal son' and 'a paralytic healed'. What a contrast to other stories of kings and rulers! We like to read about celebrities and people who lead glamorous lives, but God often does the opposite of what we expect. God prefers to focus on ordinary people and how they become quiet heroes through loving acts of faith; God invites us to do the same.

Prayer: *God of all people, help us to look beyond earthly success. Open our eyes to see the value of all people, just as you do. Amen.*

Thought for the day: God exalts those who act with faith.

Bob LaForge (New Jersey, USA)

Christmas all year

Read Matthew 1:18–25
They will call him, Emmanuel. (Emmanuel means 'God with us.')
Matthew 1:23 (CEB)

For Christmas last year we received a clock that chimes the tune of a Christmas hymn every hour on the hour. We enjoyed listening to the clock throughout Advent and Christmas. In the new year, I took down the clock and was ready to store it until the following Christmas season when my husband, José, asked me not to pack it away. He thoroughly enjoyed listening to the chimes since they reminded him of the meaning of Christmas.

At first I thought it odd listening to Christmas melodies in March and June and September. But the reason to celebrate Christmas – the coming of God in the flesh – is the foundation of our faith and our reason to live every single day of the year. Throughout the year we do not know what situations we will encounter. Some will be agreeable; others will not.

But the gospel message in Matthew of the birth of the child Jesus, 'Emmanuel', reassures us that God is always with us, throughout the year.

Prayer: *God of infinite goodness, thank you for walking with us every day of the year. Amen.*

Thought for the day: The birth of Jesus promises that God is with me – every day of the year.

Priscila Laguna (Puebla, México)

How to write for *The Upper Room*

The meditations in each issue of *The Upper Room* are written by people just like you. Here are some guidelines for submitting your story:

- Make only one point.
- Include details about what you heard, saw, felt or said.
- Tell about your own experience and the spiritual truth you learned from it.
- Include a suggested Bible reading, scripture verse, prayer and thought for the day. These should relate to the point of your meditation.

Further guidance on writing for *The Upper Room* can be found at **submissions.upperroom.org/en/guidelines**

Meditations for the UK edition of *The Upper Room* may be submitted by email to **theupperroom@brf.org.uk** or by post to:

The Upper Room
BRF
15 The Chambers
Vineyard
Abingdon OX14 3FE

If submitting by post, please still include a contact email address, if possible. We will notify you if we choose to publish your work.

Meditations submitted without contact information will not be considered for publication.

Quiet comfort

Read Job 1:13–22

[Job's friends] sat with him on the ground seven days and seven nights, and no one spoke a word to him, for they saw that his suffering was very great.
Job 2:13 (NRSV)

As my grandfather's health began declining, I visited him often. When my extended family heard his health had taken a turn for the worse, they all flew into town to see him. This ensured that he would never be alone. We sat in his hospice room in silence, day and night, praying he would get better.

During this time, I thought about Job. Even after deep loss he remained faithful and praised God. In Job 2:13, Job's friends came to visit him. They sat beside him for seven days and nights in silence, comforting him without using words. Quiet comfort can be the best gift for a grieving or hurt person. In times where sorrow is too deep for words, the act of just being with the person speaks volumes.

The days of silence and comfort helped Job process and deal with his sadness, while having the support he needed. Sometimes we feel we cannot comfort someone who is experiencing great grief or sorrow because we don't know what to say; but in difficult times, silent companionship is a good way to remind others that they are loved.

Prayer: *Dear Lord, help us remember that you are always with us and that we can feel your love through the companionship of others. Amen.*

Thought for the day: My presence can remind others that God loves them.

Paul Farley (North Carolina, USA)

A good Samaritan

Read Luke 10:25–37

[The lawyer] answered, 'You shall love the Lord your God with all your heart and with all your soul and with all your strength and with all your mind and your neighbour as yourself.'
Luke 10:27 (NRSV)

When I was a child I enjoyed spending time in my father's tailor shop, listening to him tell stories from his childhood while he worked. My father was happy growing up in Armenia until war broke out in 1915. He was forced to flee his home; he stayed on the move – walking by day, hiding among the trees by night.

One day while he was walking down a road, he saw a group of boys heading his way, intent on harming him because he was Armenian and Christian. My father scrambled into a ditch, raised his arms and cried, 'Dear God, save me!' In desperation, he waved down a passing car. The driver stopped, told him to get into the car and asked, 'Where are you going?' My father stammered, 'Anywhere.'

The man took him to an inn and gave him fresh clothes. That night my father bathed, ate a good meal and slept at the inn. The following day my father wanted to thank the man, but he was gone. He had paid for the night's stay and left some money for my father. Who was this man? My father never found out.

This stranger lived out the parable of the good Samaritan, caring for my father even though he was a stranger. We can all learn from the kindness this man showed and remember that we have the ability to show love and mercy to others as well.

Prayer: *Merciful God, thank you for watching over us in unexpected ways and through the people you send into our lives. Amen.*

Thought for the day: Whom is God calling me to help today?

Rebeca Boyadjian (Montevideo, Uruguay)

PRAYER FOCUS: THOSE SUFFERING PERSECUTION

Freedom!

Read Exodus 6:1–7

It is for freedom that Christ has set us free. Stand firm, then, and do not let yourselves be burdened again by a yoke of slavery.
Galatians 5:1 (NIV)

As a black man living in the United States, I consider freedom one of my most precious blessings. My ancestors were slaves once, bought and sold like property, worked like cattle and sometimes beaten even to the point of death.

My ancestors could only dream of the freedom I was born with. It is never far from my thoughts that if I had been born 200 years ago, I couldn't do any of the things I am doing with my life today. I am a free man, and no matter how busy or stressed I get, I always take time to cherish and give thanks for this powerful truth.

Free. We use the word carelessly, often for food we didn't pay for or two-for-one sales that give us even more stuff we don't really need. Yet the power in that word should never be underestimated. I was born free. Maybe that's why, when the word of God tells me that all people every-where were born into slavery to selfishness and sin and that Jesus died to set us free, I can barely choke back the tears. Each of us wore shackles around our necks, powerless against sin and death. And because Christ died for us, the chains are removed and we are let go – free to believe in, trust and follow Jesus.

Prayer: *Dear Jesus, thank you for giving your life to set us free. Help us to share this gift with all those who are still in bondage. Amen.*

Thought for the day: Freedom from sin and death is a true treasure from God.

Gary Mitchell (North Carolina, USA)

Even me

Read Matthew 6:25–33

God so loved the world that he gave his one and only Son, that whoever believes in him shall not perish but have eternal life.
John 3:16 (NIV)

I've always had to work really hard in school. I make many mistakes, and my dad has to point them out and explain them to me. I was so discouraged by my struggles with school that I began to feel that I didn't deserve any of the good things in my life.

When I expressed my feelings of unworthiness, my dad explained that God may give us challenging tasks but also will help us through them. Dad reminded me of this verse: 'Look at the birds of the air; they do not sow or reap or store away in barns, and yet your heavenly Father feeds them. Are you not much more valuable than they?' (Matthew 6:26). I thought, *How good those birds have it; they don't have to go to school and God still takes care of them!* Then Dad read John 3:16 to me, to remind me how much God loves me.

Even when I mess up, God still gives me oxygen, sunshine, food and many other good things just because God loves each of us so very much. Now I do my work with more enthusiasm because I know that even when I make mistakes, God is with me and still loves me.

Prayer: *Dear God, thank you for caring for us, even when we feel we don't deserve it. In the name of Jesus Christ. Amen.*

Thought for the day: I don't have to do anything to earn God's love.

David Serdyukov (Moscow, Russia)

Ebenezer

Read 1 Samuel 7:8–12

Samuel took a stone… and named it Ebenezer; for he said, 'Thus far the Lord has helped us.'
1 Samuel 7:12 (NRSV)

When I first sang the words, 'Here I raise my Ebenezer; hither by thy help I'm come,'* I had no idea what 'Ebenezer' meant. Then I read today's scripture and learned that Ebenezer refers to a stone memorial that Samuel built to remind the people how much God had helped them. The word means 'Stone of Help.'

I recognise the Lord's daily help when I look back at my journals, which I now think of as 'Ebenezer journals'. Each day I make a list of ten things I am thankful for from the day before. I also make a list of prayer requests. The thank-you lists are often answers to the requests. No matter the year or date, as I flip open the pages I am always struck by God's faithfulness. I am especially thankful for these records on days when I question God's answers – or lack of answers.

When we remember God's help 'thus far', then, like Samuel, we can give thanks. And as we raise our Ebenezers, we need not doubt that help will come.

Prayer: *Loving Father, thank you for hearing our prayers. Help us to trust your faithfulness. Amen.*

Thought for the day: What can I use as a reminder of God's faithfulness?

* From the hymn 'Come, thou fount of every blessing' by Robert Robinson (1735–90).

Deb Vellines (Missouri, USA)

God listens

Read Ephesians 6:18–20
The prayer of a righteous person is powerful and effective.
James 5:16 (NIV)

In February 2016 I was sentenced to jail, a new and unexpected experience for me, after having served my country as a soldier and my community as a firefighter. In June 2017, I began sharing a cell with an older man who explained to me the message of the gospel. Seven days later, I accepted Jesus as my Saviour. As my cellmate and I prayed and studied each day, I began to experience God's love in amazing ways.

My new friend gave me a Bible with James 5:16 highlighted. The next day he was told he would be transferred to another jail, so we both prayed fervently that he would not be moved. The day he was to leave, the transfer was cancelled. But then, three weeks later, my friend was sent to another jail. Instead of being angry with God for separating us, I kept reading God's word and prayed constantly that it would be God's will to bring us back together again.

Twelve days later, he and I were both transferred – to the same jail – and we were cellmates once again. God truly answered our prayers in the way that we had hoped. Now we have a daily fellowship group with several other inmates. Every time our group is together, we pray for each other.

Prayer: *Faithful God, whenever we are lost and depressed from our trials, give us strength. Amen.*

Thought for the day: Every day, I pray for the Lord's will to be done.

Aaron Priest (New South Wales, Australia)

Hospitality to strangers

Read Hebrews 13:1–3

Do not forget to show hospitality to strangers, for by so doing some
people have shown hospitality to angels without knowing it.
Hebrews 13:2 (NIV)

After a very long flight, I emerged from the Paris Metro car feeling weary.
I struggled with the two large pieces of luggage I had brought with me.
An escalator surely must be nearby, I thought. But as I turned the corner,
I sighed and dropped my bags. The escalator was out of service. Rush hour
was just beginning and hundreds of Parisians passed me by, hurrying to
their destinations, never even noticing, or perhaps irritated, that I had
stopped in their path. Suddenly I felt someone reaching for the bag on my
right. When I realised the woman was reaching not to steal my bag but to
carry it for me, I grabbed the other bag and together we made the trek.

My good Samaritan was a young Muslim woman wearing a hijab.
When we reached the tree-lined avenue outside the metro station, she
left my bag and proceeded on her way. All I could do was yell, '*Shukran!*'
the Arabic word for 'Thank you'.

This woman saw my need and met it. Her action reminded me that
no matter who we are, where we come from or the basis of our faith,
in the end we are all God's children. Her kindness inspired me to show
hospitality to friends and strangers alike.

Prayer: *Dear God, help us to exercise our privilege of service to meet*
the needs of all your children. Amen.

Thought for the day: Today I will offer godly hospitality to strangers
in my path.

Teresa Cannaday (Florida, USA)

Starting over

Read Matthew 4:18–22

'Come, follow me,' Jesus said, 'and I will send you out to fish for people.'
Matthew 4:19 (NIV)

Anytime we start over again, whether it's a new career or a new way of life, we need to invest a great deal of time and attention if our new path is to be successful.

Jesus Christ offers us all a new start, with a special invitation to leave behind our investment in worldly cares and follow him. Jesus gave this same invitation to his first disciples, Simon and Andrew, who were fishermen. 'Come, follow me,' Jesus said, 'and I will send you out to fish for people.'

I remember the Lord calling me in much the same way. I was beginning to realise that I could not handle my life by myself; I needed some faithful companion who would support me in both good days and bad. It was then that God called me – through my students, who invited me to their home and told me about Jesus, the companion I so dearly needed. From then on I have invested my time and attention in God's kingdom. I am trying to share the good news of God's love with those who need desperately to hear it.

With Christ as our companion, we can throw our nets in new directions and with deep dedication begin or continue our special calling to fish for people by living lives of compassion and love.

Prayer: *Dear God, teach us to invest who we are and what we have for the good of your people everywhere. Thank you for inviting us into your kingdom. Amen.*

Thought for the day: New life in Christ means new commitment.

Ratna Chapagain (Kathmandu, Nepal)

Never in vain

Read Romans 1:8–17

Let us not become weary in doing good, for at the proper time we will reap a harvest if we do not give up.
Galatians 6:9 (NIV)

'Hi. It's Bonnie,' said the voice on the phone. 'I just wanted you to know that I've come back to the Lord.' The ring of excitement in her voice when she said these words identified her as the Bonnie who once attended a Bible study I'd taught. Bonnie asked to come over to my house to tell me more.

That afternoon, her voice rang with joy as she told me of her ministry with people new to Canada. 'And you won't believe this, but I'm helping with a ladies' Bible study.' Women from many countries now gather in Bonnie's living room to study God's word.

Bonnie's story warmed my heart and reminded me that the time and energy I had spent in our Bible study mattered. When things or people don't turn out as we'd hoped, we may feel as if our work has been in vain. We may even become discouraged and give up. But that day, I learned that nothing we do in the name of Jesus is meaningless. If we do not lose heart and give up, then someday when we've forgotten our efforts or written them off as a loss, our 'reward' may just ring the doorbell and tell us stories of grace that will fill our hearts with praise.

Prayer: *Dear Lord, help us to stay faithful in the work you've given us, always remembering its eternal value. Amen.*

Thought for the day: My efforts for the Lord are never in vain.

Rose McCormick Brandon (Ontario, Canada)

BRF's Bible reading notes are published three times a year in January, May and September, and provide daily encouragement and hope for the Christian journey. You can order individual copies or subscribe from most Christian bookshops or directly from BRF.

New Daylight is our most popular series written for everyone on their daily journey with God.

Guidelines is our series of Bible reading notes for church leaders, students and those seeking to interpret and apply the biblical text with confidence in today's world.

The Upper Room is written by its readers all over the world and focuses on finding God in daily experience.

Day by Day with God is our series written for women, by women who have themselves found the Bible a source of strength and inspiration for life.

Bible Reflections for Older People seeks to bring hope, assurance and sustenance to the older reader.

To order your subscription use the order form overleaf, go to **brfonline.org.uk** or telephone the BRF office on +44 (0)1865 319700, Monday to Friday, 9.30 am to 5.00 pm.

THE UPPER ROOM: INDIVIDUAL/GIFT SUBSCRIPTION FORM

> **All our Bible reading notes can be ordered online by visiting brfonline.org.uk/subscriptions**

☐ I would like to take out a subscription myself (complete your name and address details once)

☐ I would like to give a gift subscription (please provide both names and addresses)

Title .... First name/initials .... Surname ....

Address ....

.... Postcode ....

Telephone .... Email ....

Gift subscription name ....

Gift subscription address ....

.... Postcode ....

Gift message (20 words max. or include your own gift card):

....

....

Please send *The Upper Room* beginning with the January 2024 / May 2024 / September 2024 issue (*delete as appropriate*):

Annual individual subscription ☐ £19.50

Optional donation to support the work of BRF £ ....

Total enclosed £ .... (cheques should be made payable to 'BRF')

Method of payment

Please charge my MasterCard / Visa with £ ....

Card no. ☐☐☐☐ ☐☐☐☐ ☐☐☐☐ ☐☐☐☐

Expires end ☐☐ ☐☐   Security code ☐☐☐   Last 3 digits on the reverse of the card

URIN